To Clementine Hollyer

GEMINI

A guide to living your best astrological life

STELLA ANDROMEDA

ILLUSTRATED BY EVI O. STUDIO

Hardie Grant

BOOKS

III.
Give Me More

Introduction

Inscribed on the forecourt of the ancient Greek temple of Apollo at Delphi are the words 'know thyself'. This is one of the 147 Delphic maxims, or rules to live by, attributed to Apollo himself, and was later extended by the philosopher Socrates to the sentence, 'The unexamined life is not worth living.'

People seek a variety of ways of knowing themselves, of coming to terms with life and trying to find ways to understand the challenges of human existence, often through therapy or belief systems like organised religion. These are ways in which we strive to understand the relationships we have with ourselves and others better, seeking out particular tools that enable us to do so.

As far as systems of understanding human nature and experience go, astrology has much to offer through its symbolic use of the constellations of the heavens, the depictions of the zodiac signs, the planets and their energetic effects. Many people find accessing this information and harnessing its potential a useful way of thinking about how to manage their lives more effectively.

What is astrology?

In simple terms, astrology is the study and interpretation of how the planets can influence us, and the world in which we live, through an understanding of their positions at a specific place in time. The practice of astrology relies on a combination of factual knowledge of the characteristics of these positions and their psychological interpretation.

Astrology is less of a belief system and more of a tool for living, from which ancient and established wisdom can be drawn. Any of us can learn to use astrology, not so much for divination or telling the future, but as a guidebook that provides greater insight and a more thoughtful way of approaching life. Timing is very much at the heart of astrology, and knowledge of planetary configurations and their relationship to each other at specific moments in time can assist in helping us with the timing of some of our life choices and decisions.

Knowing when major life shifts can occur – because of particular planetary configurations such as a Saturn return (see page 103) or Mercury retrograde (see page 104) – or what it means to have Venus in your seventh house (see pages 85 and 98), while recognising the specific characteristics of your sign, are all tools that you can use to your advantage. Knowledge is power, and astrology can be a very powerful supplement to approaching life's ups and downs and any relationships we form along the way.

The 12 signs of the zodiac

Each sign of the zodiac has a range of recognisable characteristics, shared by people born under that sign. This is your Sun sign, which you probably already know – and the usual starting point from which we each begin to explore our own astrological paths. Sun sign characteristics can be strongly exhibited in an individual's make-up; however, this is only part of the picture.

Usually, how we appear to others is tempered by the influence of other factors – and these are worth bearing in mind. Your ascendant sign is equally important, as is the positioning of your Moon. You can also look to your opposite sign to see what your Sun sign may need a little more of, to balance its characteristics.

After getting to know your Sun sign in the first part of this book, you might want to dive into the Give Me More section (see pages 74–105) to start to explore all the particulars of your birth chart. These will give you far greater insight into the myriad astrological influences that may play out in your life.

Sun signs

It takes 365 (and a quarter, to be precise) days for the Earth to orbit the Sun and in so doing, the Sun appears to us to spend a month travelling through each sign of the zodiac. Your Sun sign is therefore an indication of the sign that the Sun was travelling through at the time of your birth. Knowing what Sun signs you and your family, friends and lovers are provides you with just the beginning of the insights into character and personality that astrology can help you discover.

On the cusp

For those for whom a birthday falls close to the end of one Sun sign and the beginning of another, it's worth knowing what time you were born. There's no such thing, astrologically, as being 'on the cusp' – because the signs begin at a specific time on a specific date, although this can vary a little year on year. If you are not sure, you'll need to know your birth date, birth time and birth place to work out accurately to which Sun sign you belong. Once you have these, you can consult an astrologer or run your details through an online astrology site program (see page 108) to give you the most accurate birth chart possible.

Taurus

The bull

21 APRIL–20 MAY

Grounded, sensual and appreciative
of bodily pleasures, Taurus is a fixed
earth sign endowed by its ruling
planet Venus with grace and a love
of beauty, despite its depiction
as a bull. Generally characterised
by an easy and uncomplicated, if
occasionally stubborn, approach to
life, Taurus' opposite sign is
watery Scorpio.

Aries

The ram

21 MARCH–20 APRIL

Astrologically the first sign of the
zodiac, Aries appears alongside the
vernal (or spring) equinox. A cardinal
fire sign, depicted by the ram, it is
the sign of beginnings and ruled
by planet Mars, which represents a
dynamic ability to meet challenges
energetically and creatively. Its
opposite sign is airy Libra.

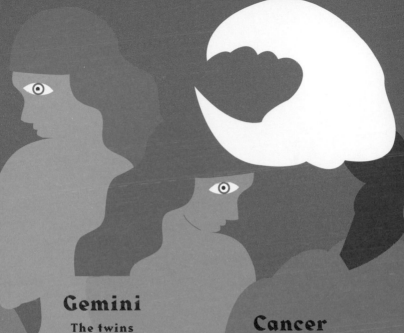

Gemini

The twins

✳

21 MAY–20 JUNE

A mutable air sign symbolised by the twins, Gemini tends to see both sides of an argument, its speedy intellect influenced by its ruling planet Mercury. Tending to fight shy of commitment, this sign also epitomises a certain youthfulness of attitude. Its opposite sign is fiery Sagittarius.

Cancer

The crab

✳

21 JUNE–21 JULY

Depicted by the crab and the tenacity of its claws, Cancer is a cardinal water sign, emotional and intuitive, its sensitivity protected by its shell. Ruled by the maternal Moon, the shell also represents the security of home, to which Cancer is committed. Its opposite sign is earthy Capricorn.

Leo
The lion

22 JULY–21 AUGUST

A fixed fire sign, ruled by the Sun, Leo loves to shine and is an idealist at heart, positive and generous to a fault. Depicted by the lion, Leo can roar with pride and be confident and uncompromising, with a great faith and trust in humanity. Its opposite sign is airy Aquarius.

Virgo
The virgin
★

22 AUGUST–21 SEPTEMBER

Traditionally represented as a maiden or virgin, this mutable earth sign is observant, detail oriented and tends towards self-sufficiency. Ruled by Mercury, Virgos benefit from a sharp intellect that can be self-critical, while often being very health conscious. Its opposite sign is watery Pisces.

Scorpio

The scorpion

✳

22 OCTOBER–21 NOVEMBER

Given to intense feelings, as befits a fixed water sign, Scorpio is depicted by the scorpion – linking it to the rebirth that follows death – and is ruled by both Pluto and Mars. With a strong spirituality and deep emotions, Scorpio needs security to transform its strength. Its opposite sign is earthy Taurus.

Libra

The scales

✳

22 SEPTEMBER–21 OCTOBER

A cardinal air sign, ruled by Venus, Libra is all about beauty, balance (as depicted by the scales) and harmony in its rather romanticised, ideal world. With a strong aesthetic sense, Libra can be both arty and crafty, but also likes fairness and can be very diplomatic. Its opposite sign is fiery Aries.

Sagittarius
The archer
✴
22 NOVEMBER–21 DECEMBER

Depicted by the archer, Sagittarius is a mutable fire sign that's all about travel and adventure, in body or mind, and is very direct in approach. Ruled by the benevolent Jupiter, Sagittarius is optimistic with lots of ideas; liking a free rein, but with a tendency to generalise. Its opposite sign is airy Gemini.

Capricorn
The goat
✴
22 DECEMBER–20 JANUARY

Ruled by Saturn, Capricorn is a cardinal earth sign associated with hard work and depicted by the sure-footed and sometimes playful goat. Trustworthy and unafraid of commitment, Capricorn is often very self-sufficient and has the discipline for the freelance working life. Its opposite sign is the watery Cancer.

Pisces
The fish
✱
20 FEBRUARY–20 MARCH

Acutely responsive to its surroundings, Pisces is a mutable water sign depicted by two fish, swimming in opposite directions, sometimes confusing fantasy with reality. Ruled by Neptune, its world is fluid, imaginative and empathetic, often picking up on the moods of others. Its opposite sign is earthy Virgo.

Aquarius
The water carrier
✱
21 JANUARY–19 FEBRUARY

Confusingly, given its depiction by the water carrier, Aquarius is a fixed air sign ruled by the unpredictable Uranus, sweeping away old ideas with innovative thinking. Tolerant, open-minded and all about humanity, its vision is social with a conscience. Its opposite sign is fiery Leo.

Get to

I.

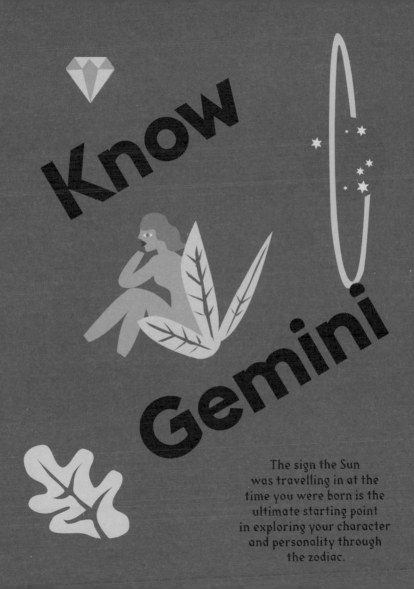

Know

Gemini

The sign the Sun
was travelling in at the
time you were born is the
ultimate starting point
in exploring your character
and personality through
the zodiac.

Mutable air sign,
depicted by the twins.

Ruled by Mercury, the
planet associated with the
messenger of the gods, linked
to communication and travel.

OPPOSITE SIGN

Sagittarius

STATEMENT OF SELF

'I think.'

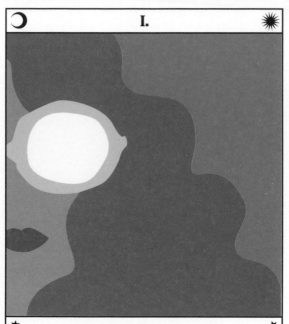

Lucky colour

Yellow, the colour of sunshine, and those nearby citrusy colours of orange and even lime green, resonating with the spark and illumination of quick-witted Mercury. Wear these colours and connect with your Gemini energy when you need a psychological boost and additional courage, choosing accessories – shoes, gloves, socks, hat or even underwear – if you don't have other clothes in these colours.

Lucky day

Wednesday. The middle of the working week for most of us, this links to the old-English deity Woden, so it's actually Woden's day, or *Wōdnesdæg*. Woden's Roman equivalent is the Mercury of Gemini influence, which we see more obviously in the French for Wednesday, *Mercredi*.

Lucky gem

Agate, a multi-coloured stone that encourages eloquence of expression and is also said to be lucky for travellers. Another Gemini gem is the citrine (from the French for lemon, *citron*) with its yellow sparkle, and yellow sapphires, which are said to stimulate the intellect.

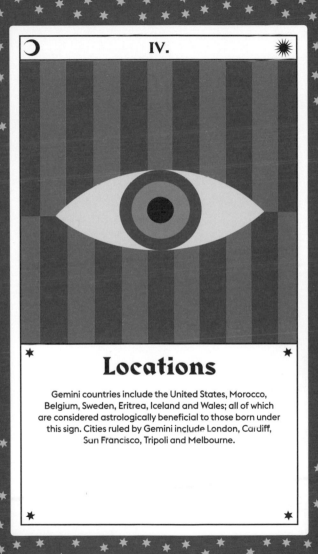

Locations

Gemini countries include the United States, Morocco, Belgium, Sweden, Eritrea, Iceland and Wales; all of which are considered astrologically beneficial to those born under this sign. Cities ruled by Gemini include London, Cardiff, San Francisco, Tripoli and Melbourne.

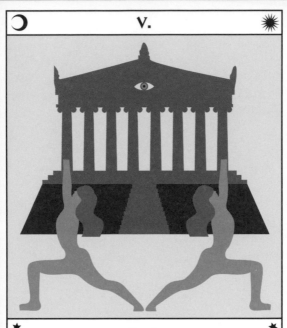

Holidays

Gemini loves to travel as long as their lively mind
is stimulated, so holiday destinations often include sights
and sounds to invigorate their body and mind. This could
be taking in the architecture of Rome or visiting the Greek
temples on the island of Sicily, watching the light show
of the *aurorae borealis* in Iceland or marvelling at
the flower markets of Hong Kong.

Flowers

Lavender's invigorating scent refreshes and calms the busy Gemini mind, while the delicate lily of the valley brings Gemini good luck. Azaleas, too, with their burst of bright colour, are also a Gemini flower.

Trees

Acacia and mimosa, with their airy leaves and delicately scented, yellow flowers, are Gemini trees. According to the bible, the wood of the acacia was used to build the Ark of the Covenant, giving it additional significance and meaning.

Pets

As might be expected of an air sign, a bird is an attractive
pet for Gemini. Either a parrot with iridescent green
feathers or a cockatiel with its beautiful bright-eyed
and inquiring look and gift for verbal mimicry, a bit like
Gemini themselves. Both birds are easily trained
to be good companions.

Parties

The first to arrive, the last to leave, this airy, communicative sign is an astrological party animal. Large gatherings in which to mingle and chat and dance until sunrise appeal to Gemini's gregarious nature – as long as there are people, then the location, food and drink are pretty immaterial. When it comes to cocktails, a dry martini suits their sophisticated wit and is often a favourite.

Gemini
characteristics

The key words for Gemini are airy, communicative, versatile, energetic in mind and adaptable by nature. There's something quixotic, mercurial, about them, too, which fascinates others. Occasionally rather lax or discreet about the truth of a situation, this is less about deliberately lying as skirting around the issue when it suits them. Sometimes considered rather capricious as a consequence, there is a duality to Gemini's make-up, depicted in its representation by the mythological twins, Castor and Pollus, born of the same mother but two different fathers.

This duality can be seen in an ability to assume two (or even more) roles, made possible by an easy adaptability because Gemini is a mutable sign. This can also make Gemini restless, seeing them flit from one idea, one role, or job, or occupation, to another; a sort of hyperactivity that can result in a dissipation of energy. All of which can lend superficiality to Gemini dealings with others, as each new idea seems to spark another and another and another – making it hard for anyone else to keep up. Gemini ideas are often good, but unless they are delivered on, nothing will stick, and to be successful, this is a lesson useful for Gemini to learn.

Ruled by Mercury, Gemini's urge to communicate is open to view, as even if not speaking, they're likely to be messaging, texting, emailing or surfing social media – often doing many of these simultaneously. Gemini always has an opinion and something interesting to say, making new and unusual connections between ideas, and their sharp observations make them an entertaining companion. Because of this facility, public engagement holds little anxiety and talking to strangers is positively relished. Even shy Geminis find that their innate curiosity about life helps them overcome barriers to connection. Gemini is also likely to have a wide range of friends and companions, often from markedly different walks of life, which reflects their chameleon-like tendency to adapt to their surroundings.

There's also a super-rational and emotionally distant side to Gemini, something that can make them very good at arguing a position, because their quick minds are able to see different perspectives without confusing the argument. This rationality can also mean, however, that it's not always easy for Gemini to think or feel deeply and if this goes unaddressed it can create problems in relationships.

TEMPERING THE AIR

The key characteristics of any Sun sign can be balanced out (or sometimes reinforced) by the characteristics of other signs in the same birth chart, particularly those of the ascendant and the Moon. So if someone doesn't appear to be typical of their Sun sign, that's why. However, those nascent Gemini aspects will always be there as a key influence, informing an individual's approach to life.

Physical Gemini

Gemini often looks younger than their years, with a bright energetic look in their eye and a physicality that keeps them light of foot and very active into old age. They have a sort of Peter Pan approach to life that's played out in their youthful appearance and they often go to some lengths to resist the ageing process and maintain their more superficial attractiveness – as long as this can be done, often literally, on the run. They don't have time to waste on endless grooming.

Health

The hands, arms and shoulders, from which their metaphorical wings can make them airborne, are the points at which Gemini is susceptible to health problems, and injuries can include repetitive strain (RSI) from long hours spent communicating via a computer keyboard and mouse. Those organs also linked to air and inspiration, the lungs, can show a weakness too and be susceptible to problems including asthma, bronchitis and pneumonia. With their tendency towards a speedy lifestyle, eating properly and nutritiously may be low down on the list of Gemini priorities and while this can keep them physically slim, their nutritional intake may actually be poor and contribute to general health problems in the long run.

Exercise

Keeping the muscles of the arms, shoulders and upper back strong can be helpful in preventing tendonitis and repetitive strain injuries. This also helps maintain a good posture, which will improve lung function too. Gyms can be attractive to Gemini because of their social aspect, but they tend to prefer a quick routine that serves its immediate purpose before they rush off to the next thing that has grabbed their attention. They tend to be dexterous and well co-ordinated, favouring sports that focus on hand-eye coordination, like tennis or golf.

How Gemini communicates

In short, fast and furious sums up the Gemini mode of communication, even at the keyboard. Their speaking voice can often be breathy and light, in keeping with their airy Sun sign, but clear and well enunciated: they don't mumble. However, what they communicate either verbally or in writing may appear to lack immediate substance or explanation. It's not that they are thoughtless, it's just that Gemini thinking is so quick, they sometimes fail to communicate what is so obvious to them, but which isn't quite as clear to others. It's a good idea for speedy Gemini to remember that it is often this which makes it necessary for others to ask for clarification, not that the rest of the world is thick or slow.

Gemini careers

Given their obvious relish in the art of communication, rational thought and the ability to hold numerous ideas in mind at the same time, it should come as no surprise that barristers are often Geminis. Relying on the ability to think on their feet, Gemini's key attributes serve them well in the theatre of the court room. That airy rhetoric can also be the sign of the wheeler dealer or politician.

Journalism in print or broadcast form is a typically Gemini occupation, particularly because of the very transitory nature of its existence. Writing books tends to require more tenacity and persistence than many Geminis possess but, if harnessed, their ability with words can be used to write both fact or fiction.

A love of travel might mean working as a tour guide suits Gemini, incorporating their love of sharing knowledge, visiting foreign places and being around people.

How Gemini chimes

Often blessed with many friends from a variety of different backgrounds, Gemini is a gregarious and outgoing type, having an easy ability to mingle and mix with a diverse crowd. This makes them a popular friend, but they can be hard to pin down, the proverbial butterfly flitting from relationship to relationship, sometimes finding it hard to commit. This is less to do with wilfulness but more a sort of habitual desire to be on the move and to travel lightly. It may take someone who understands the Gemini dynamic to convince them of the value of commitment and that the security of a relationship needn't tie them down but could instead provide a safe place from which to travel and return.

The Gemini woman

The Gemini woman is a bit of a flirt by nature, and resistant to being tied down. This airy spirit needs her wings on which to fly, so any attempts to clip them could find her gone. She uses her hands to communicate in conversation, but isn't particularly touchy-feely, meaning she can convey an air of reserve. Because of this, although she's friendly, she often appears to maintain a slight distance.

NOTABLE GEMINI WOMEN

Joan Collins, with her continuing youthful appearance, exudes a slightly reserved aura, while her sense of drama is communicated through her style. Tennis champion Venus Williams shows the strength in her Gemini arms as an exceptional athlete, along with fellow tennis player Steffi Graff. Judy Garland communicated with her voice, while actresses Marilyn Monroe, Angelina Jolie and Nicole Kidman all share the graceful but mercurial Gemini allure.

The Gemini man

The Gemini man often looks younger than his age, and this can make his sophisticated ideas something of a surprise – he's not to be underestimated. His ability to surf friendships, or to keep them at arm's length, makes him difficult to pin down and he can make several arrangements for the same time, then decline them all for another that's just cropped up. Infuriatingly, he's such a charmer he usually gets away with it.

Who love

whom?

Gemini & Aries

Gemini's air gives oxygen to Aries' fire, and this is a free-spirited but hot-blooded combination that relies on friendship as much as lust. As long as Aries' decisiveness doesn't feel restrictive to Gemini, this can be a successful pairing.

Gemini & Taurus

Gemini can find the uncomplicated approach of this earth sign fascinating but not particularly compelling, and is likely to find the earthy Taurus a tad unchallenging for their more adventurous tastes.

Gemini & Gemini

Twins meet twins, so they recognise each other, but this double dual combination might prove just too frenetic and flighty to last the course, especially when the relationship moves out of the bedroom.

Gemini &
Cancer

Gemini's playfulness might
prove too much for Cancer's
need for security. Not knowing
quite what's going on is the
wind beneath Gemini's wings,
but can be just too volatile
for this sensitive sign, who
prefers calmer waters.

Gemini & Leo

There's a good union to be
enjoyed between these two
outgoing, confident signs given
to playful extroversion, both in
and out of bed. But Leo's need
to always be number one in
Gemini's life may prove tricky
to accommodate.

Gemini & Virgo

Given they are both ruled by
Mercury there's an initial mental
affinity between them, but Gemini
tends to find Virgo's detail-focused
approach pernickety and boring, often
making this a spiky combination
from the word go.

Gemini &
Scorpio

There's immediate passion in the bedroom, but a problem outside it because Gemini's share-all nature conflicts with Scorpio's need for privacy. Unless this clash is managed with tact on both sides, it can herald the end before it starts.

Gemini &
Libra

Intellectually, these two air signs create a lovely harmony. They are generally in agreement with each other and share a taste for travel and entertainment. Well matched sexually, there's a tolerance and ease that suits them both.

Gemini &
Sagittarius

They are each other's opposite sign, so the attraction is there and it's strong between their bodies and minds, but both are restless by nature and if this isn't recognised, it can inhibit any commitment between the two of them.

Gemini &
Aquarius

Because both share an airy, innovative
approach to life and an inclination
to unpredictability, this is an easy
combination with an affection and
appreciation for each other that can
forge a happy and enduring bond.

Gemini &
Pisces

There's lots of passion to be had here
and it creates a potent attraction
initially, but airy Gemini really doesn't
understand Pisces' imagination and
sensitivity and has a tendency to be
irritated by their need for security.

Gemini &
Capricorn

The promise of order holds some
attraction and this steadying
influence can be good for
Gemini, while Capricorn's
sombre side can be lightened
in return. It's a question of
balance, though, and to reach
that takes patience and tact.

Gemini love-o-meter

Least compatible

Virgo   Cancer   Gemini   Taurus   Pisces   Scorpio

Most compatible

Leo   Sagittarius   Aries   Capricorn   Aquarius   Libra

The Gemini

II.

Deep Dive

In this section, dive deeper into the ways in which your Sun sign might be driving you or holding you back, and start to think about how you might use this knowledge to inform your path.

The
Gemini
home

Gemini security doesn't particularly lie in bricks and mortar, so they are one of the signs most likely to instigate regular house moves, or constant change and redecoration within the home. What is important to them, though, is to have a home that is light and airy and doesn't contain too much clutter. Not exactly minimalist, there is a Gemini tendency to create large, open-plan spaces where they feel they can breathe – and they are not averse to high-rise accommodation, either. The colour of the decor may be Geminian, on the yellow and light green spectrum, but there's also likely to be a lot of white and pale blue-sky colours, reminiscent of the air. At the first sight of sunshine, windows are likely to be flung open and the door is often left ajar, inviting in guests, friends and strangers alike.

It is likely there will be lots of books or magazines and other reading material in the Gemini home – given their tendency to flit between one thing and another, they often have several books on the go at once. You will probably also find iPads, laptops and other communication devices – with the speediest internet connectivity money can buy.

TOP TIPS FOR
GEMINI SELF-CARE

* Help that busy mind to slow
  down by learning meditation.

* Don't say yes to every invite
  and opportunity: me-time
  is invaluable.

* Slow down by regularly taking
  a walk in natural surroundings.

Self-care

Self-care isn't high on the Gemini agenda, but it's worth
taking stock and thinking about how many problems could be
avoided, reduced or eliminated if a bit more thought was given
to it. All that speedy activity can cause accidental injuries –
from falling over and spraining a wrist to slicing vegetables
so fast that fingers get cut. Hands, arms and shoulders can be
particularly susceptible to stresses and strains.

Constant rushing about can cause exhaustion, too, and
while Gemini isn't usually affected by insomnia, hyperactivity
can create havoc with sleep. Pinging awake at 3 a.m. with
a racing mind can be avoided by factoring in a bit more
downtime generally. Often, Gemini doesn't recognise this as
a problem until they almost literally keel over, becoming forced
to learn the hard way how best to avoid this. And avoiding
burnout should be a priority for this active mind, as it can
cause anxiety and depression. Luckily, Gemini tends to be
emotionally resilient and a quick learner. It's just that they
don't always seem to realise that self-care does not work as
a one-off thing but is something that has to be integrated
into daily life in order to support busy lifestyles.

WHAT TO KEEP IN THE GEMINI PANTRY

★ Eggs: quick and easy to cook, the perfect protein-packed fast food.

★ Air-dried biltong for a nutritious snack.

★ A timer: an important bit of kitchen kit for easily distracted Gemini.

Food
and
cooking

If it can't be made quickly, rustled up in a moment, then Gemini is often as happy to snack on their way out of the door as they are to cook. However, when Gemini puts their mind to it, they can concoct the most delicious recipes, with spectacular results. Their manual dexterity comes into its own when separating eggs for a meringue, thinly slicing tuna for sushi, and prepping for a dish with expertise – although there's still a chance for distraction and things can burn.

TOP TIPS FOR GEMINI'S MONEY

★ Keep track of invoicing and receipts, and your tax return will benefit.

★ Give some thought, or seek advice, about a pension plan for the future.

★ Consolidate: you don't need those six bank accounts you forgot you opened.

How Gemini handles money

Money isn't a particularly strong driver for Gemini. Validation tends to be sought in personal appreciation rather than material wealth – which they usually get plenty of because they work hard and often at multiple occupations. This lack of attachment to material wealth or possessions can mean that they spend without much thought, surprisingly, given how much they generally like to think about things. Often purchases can be an extension of their desire to communicate, so a state-of-the-art computer might feature, or travel to somewhere stimulating to their mind. This lack of general acquisitiveness, and slightly easy-come, easy-go attitude to money can also mean Gemini is generous to others.

How Gemini
handles the boss

The boss can find their Gemini employees tricky, not least because it's not always obvious which one will show up at any given time or place: the employee who is good at deadlines, the one who decided at the eleventh hour to gamble on an unconventional approach to a project, or the one disappearing across the country to pursue a new lead? This unpredictability can wreak havoc with other people's schedules and deadlines – not to mention their nerves – so even though the boss knows Gemini usually does deliver, they would like to know for sure, and when!

Valued highly for their rational way of looking at a problem, the Gemini contribution to a team can sometimes be a bit unorthodox and single-minded, with little regard for others. Bear in mind that the boss has to manage a team, which includes managing everyone's different expectations – and this needs taking into account. It will be appreciated if Gemini can acknowledge and work with this dynamic, and if they do, it will gain them brownie points that should pay off.

TOP TIPS TO
HANDLE THE BOSS

✴ Don't assume that your
  boss is a mind reader:
  keep them posted.

✴ Remember, while some work
  is just routine it may also be
  important – don't ignore
  the boring stuff.

✴ Doing things your own way
  may be fine, but it's always
  better to check.

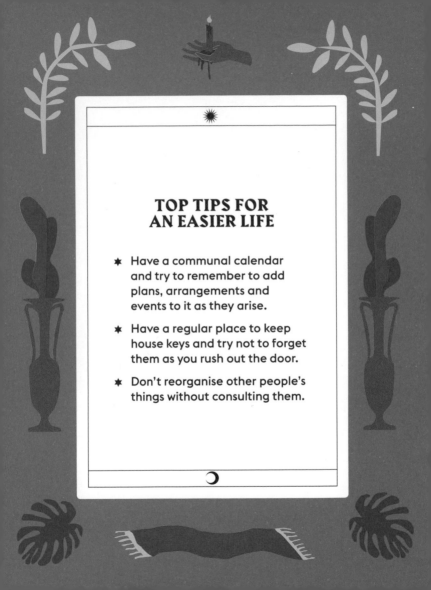

TOP TIPS FOR
AN EASIER LIFE

* Have a communal calendar
  and try to remember to add
  plans, arrangements and
  events to it as they arise.

* Have a regular place to keep
  house keys and try not to forget
  them as you rush out the door.

* Don't reorganise other people's
  things without consulting them.

What is Gemini like to live with?

If left to their own devices, Gemini is pretty easy going. Problems can arise, however, if fellow housemates or partners request some idea of what they are up to or where they are going. It's not that Gemini minds people knowing *per se*, it's just that they often haven't made up with own minds. This can make them appear rather secretive: because it's not important to them to make plans and stick to them, they can't really understand why it should matter to anyone else. However, while spontaneity and unpredictability are comfortable places for Gemini, they can be extremely disconcerting to others. It's sensible for Gemini to be mindful of this if they want to avoid alienating their housemates or partner.

Independent and outgoing, Gemini thrives on being social so are seldom holed up in their room for days on end and, as a result, their immediate domestic surroundings may be of only passing interest. An intermittent tendency to blitz through cleaning, however, may find flatmates or partner returning home to an unrecognisable space where their belongings have also been tidied up and reorganised to within an inch of their lives.

How to handle a break-up

Gemini often feels that once they've made a decision that's it, so if they have decided their relationship is completely fine, they may become so busy with other things, they misread the signs and a break-up can come as a complete surprise. Once confronted with the situation, their inclination is to rationalise and think their way through it, often refusing to consider their feelings (or anyone else's).

It's not that Gemini doesn't experience heartbreak, it's just that their strategy can be to rationalise their feelings to the point where they no longer feel them. If the boot is on the other foot, most Geminis don't vacillate but are swift executioners, even brutal, leaving no room for ambiguity. In this case, what is so obvious to *them* may come as a complete surprise to their partner. But in both cases the Gemini way is to throw it all up in the air and move on – fast.

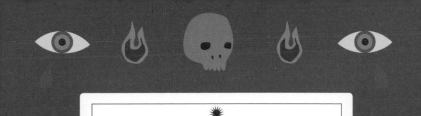

TOP TIPS FOR
AN EASIER BREAK-UP

* Apply some Gemini thought before rushing in where angels fear to tread.

* Go easy on yourself (or your ex) and allow yourself to feel and recover.

* Be a little more reflective: there may be useful lessons to be learned.

How Gemini wants to be loved

Gemini wants to be loved for who they are, body, mind and soul, but they don't always realise that it's not easy for their lover to recognise which version of their many selves has come through the door. This keeps lovers on their toes, but it is also exhausting and it's a lot to ask of a companion, so Gemini needs to be aware of this and in order to get what they need, they may need to be prepared to meet their lover half way.

In their mind, Gemini has world enough and time for languorous love-making, but the reality is that they can be so driven that love-making often gets relegated to the bottom of a list, somewhere after cleaning out the cat's litter tray to saving the world. Not very encouraging to a would-be lover, for sure, but knowing this about them means there's less likelihood of taking this predisposition quite so personally. Gemini's unpredictability about what they want and don't want can make them completely exasperating and this is a quandary for many when it comes to trying to love them. But any lover that can tactfully help Gemini take the pressure off themselves, creating some space just to *be*, will be welcomed with open arms. It's a fine balance to judge, however, and to complicate matters further this will probably only really be acceptable from a lover to whom Gemini has already made a commitment.

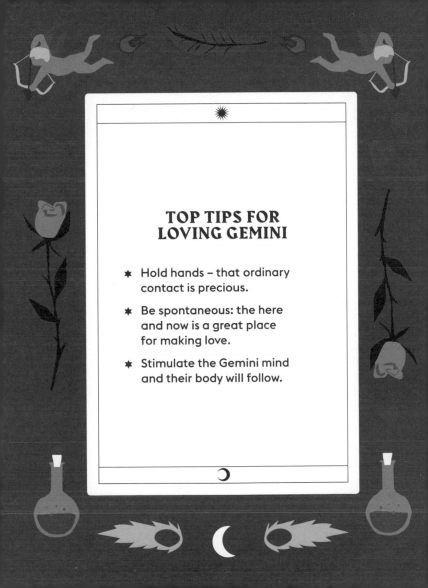

TOP TIPS FOR
LOVING GEMINI

★ Hold hands – that ordinary
  contact is precious.

★ Be spontaneous: the here
  and now is a great place
  for making love.

★ Stimulate the Gemini mind
  and their body will follow.

Gemini's sex life

Although not an overtly physical sign, Gemini loves to embrace and touch using their arms and hands and they also respond to hand, arm and shoulder massage, finding these body areas quite erotically charged. Curious, adventurous and spontaneous, they are naturally quite confident naked – sex can definitely be a light-hearted, exploratory affair for Gemini, and they are not averse to one-night stands. But while physical sex is there to be enjoyed, it is the meeting of minds that can spark sexual transcendence for Gemini. Erotic talk, too, may also feature in Gemini sex, as communicating in sound is particularly arousing and being read to can create a focus for foreplay. Role play may also be a feature of their love-making.

The downside is that in spite of their spontaneity and openness to sex *en plein air* or on the kitchen floor, as the mood takes them, Gemini is often just too fast for the more painstaking and sensual lover who can find snacking on sex, rather than making it the main course, a bit disconcerting. Staying on schedule is all very well, but Gemini could do well to remember that there are some things that benefit from being savoured occasionally, and sex is one of them.

Me & More

Your Sun sign never shows you the whole picture. In this section, learn how to read the nuances of your birth chart and discover a whole new level of astrological insight.

Your birth chart

Your birth chart is a snapshot of a particular moment, in a particular place, at the precise moment of your birth and is therefore completely individual to you. It's like a blueprint, a map, a statement of occurrence, spelling out possible traits and influences – but it isn't your destiny. It is just a symbolic tool to which you can refer, based on the position of the planets at the time of your birth. If you can't get to an astrologer, these days anyone can get their birth chart prepared in minutes online (see page 108 for a list of websites and apps that will do it for you). Even if you don't know your exact time of birth, just knowing the date and place of birth can create the beginnings of a useful template.

Remember, nothing is intrinsically good or bad in astrology and there is no explicit timing or forecasting: it's more a question of influences and how these might play out positively or negatively. And if we have some insight, and some tools with which to approach, see or interpret our circumstances and surroundings, this gives us something to work with.

When you are reading your birth chart, it's useful to first understand all the tools of astrology available to you; not only the astrological signs and what they represent, but also the 10 planets referred to in astrology and their individual characteristics, along with the 12 houses and what they mean. Individually, these tools of astrology are of passing interest, but when you start to see how they might sit in juxtaposition to each other, then the bigger picture becomes more accessible and we begin to gain insights that can be useful to us.

Broadly speaking, each of the planets suggests a different type of energy, the astrological signs propose the various ways in which that energy might be expressed, while the houses represent areas of experience in which this expression might operate.

Next to bring into the picture are the positions of the signs at four key points: the ascendant, or rising sign, and its opposite, the descendant; and the midheaven and its opposite, the IC, not to mention the different aspects created by congregations of signs and planets.

It is now possible to see how subtle the reading of a birth chart might be and how it is infinite in its variety, and highly specific to an individual. With this information, and a working understanding of the symbolic meaning and influences of the signs, planets and houses of your unique astrological profile, you can begin to use these tools to help with decision-making and other aspects of life.

Reading your chart

If you have your birth chart prepared, either by hand or via an online program, you will see a circle divided into 12 segments, with information clustered at various points indicating the position of each zodiac sign, in which segment it appears and at what degree. Irrespective of the features that are relevant to the individual, each chart follows the same pattern when it comes to interpretation.

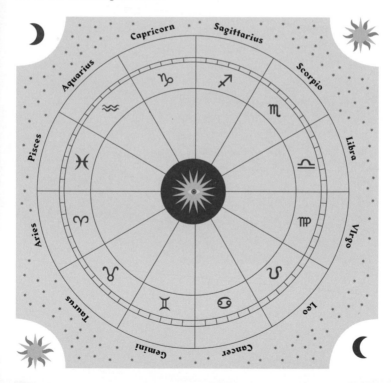

Given the time of birth, the place of birth and the position of the planets at that moment, the birth chart, sometimes called a natal horoscope, is drawn up.

If you consider the chart as a clock face, the first house (see pages 95–99 for the astrological houses) begins at the 9, and it is from this point that, travelling anti-clockwise the chart is read from the first house, through the 12 segments of the chart to the twelfth.

The beginning point, the 9, is also the point at which the Sun rises on your life, giving you your ascendant, or rising sign, and opposite to this, at the 3 of the clock face, is your descendant sign. The midheaven point of your chart, the MC, is at 12, and its opposite, the IC, at 6 (see pages 101–102).

Understanding the significance of the characteristics of the astrological signs and the planets, their particular energies, their placements and their aspects to each other can be helpful in understanding ourselves and our relationships with others. In day-to-day life, too, the changing configuration of planets and their effects are much more easily understood with a basic knowledge of astrology, as are the recurring patterns that can sometimes strengthen and sometimes delay opportunities and possibilities. Working with, rather than against, these trends can make life more manageable and, in the last resort, more successful.

The Moon effect

If your Sun sign represents your consciousness, your life force and your individual will, then the Moon represents that side of your personality that you tend to keep rather secret or hidden. This is the realm of instinct, intuition, creativity and the unconscious, which can take you places emotionally that are sometimes hard to understand. This is what brings great subtlety and nuance to a person, way beyond just their Sun sign. So you may have your Sun in Gemini, and all that means, but this might be countered by a strongly empathetic and feeling Moon in Cancer; or you may have your Sun in open-hearted Leo, but a Moon in Aquarius with all its rebellious, emotional detachment.

Phases of the Moon

The Moon orbits the Earth, taking roughly 28 days to do so. How much of the Moon we see is determined by how much of the Sun's light it reflects, giving us the impression that it waxes, or grows, and wanes. When the Moon is new, to us, only a sliver of it is illuminated. As it waxes, it reflects more light and moves from a crescent, to a waxing crescent to a first quarter; then it moves to a waxing gibbous Moon, to a full Moon. Then the Moon begins to wane through a waning gibbous, to a last quarter, and then the cycle begins again. All of this occurs over four weeks. When we have two full Moons in any one calendar month, the second is called a blue Moon.

Each month the Moon also moves through an astrological sign, as we know from our personal birth charts. This, too, will yield information – a Moon in Scorpio can have a very different effect to one in Capricorn – and depending on our personal charts, this can have a shifting influence each month. For example, if the Moon in your birth chart is in Virgo, then when the actual Moon moves into Virgo, this will have an additional influence. Read the characteristics of the signs for further information (see pages 12–17).

The Moon's cycle has an energetic effect, which we can see quite easily on the ocean tides. Astrologically, because the Moon is both a fertility symbol and attuned to our deeper psychological side, we can use this to focus more profoundly and creatively on aspects of life that are important to us.

Eclipses

Generally speaking, an eclipse covers up and prevents light being shed on a situation. Astrologically speaking, this will depend on where the Sun or Moon is positioned in relation to other planets at the time of an eclipse. So if a solar eclipse is in Gemini, there will be a Geminian influence or an influence on Geminis.

Hiding, or shedding, light on an area of our lives is an invitation to pay attention to it. Eclipses are generally about beginnings or endings, which is why our ancestors saw them as portents, important signs to be taken notice of. As it is possible to know when an eclipse is forthcoming, these are charted astronomically; consequently, their astrological significance can be assessed and acted upon ahead of time.

The 10 planets

For the purpose of astrology (but not for astronomy, because the Sun is really a star) we talk about 10 planets, and each astrological sign has a ruling planet, with Mercury, Venus and Mars each being assigned two. The characteristics of each planet describe those influences that can affect signs, all of which information feeds into the interpretation of a birth chart.

The Moon

This sign is an opposing principle to the Sun, forming a pair, and it represents the feminine, symbolising containment and receptivity, how we react most instinctively and with feeling.

Rules the sign of Cancer.

The Sun

The Sun represents the masculine, and is seen as the energy that sparks life, which suggests a paternal energy in our birth chart. It also symbolises our self or essential being, and our purpose.

Rules the sign of Leo.

Mercury

Mercury is the planet of communication and symbolises our urge to make sense of, understand and communicate our thoughts through words.

Rules the signs of Gemini and Virgo.

Venus

The planet of love is all about attraction, connection and pleasure and in a female chart it symbolises her style of femininity, while in a male chart it represents his ideal partner.

Rules the signs of Taurus and Libra.

Mars

This planet symbolises pure energy (Mars was, after all, the god of War) but it also tells you in which areas you're most likely to be assertive, aggressive or to take risks.

Rules the signs of Aries and Scorpio.

Saturn

Saturn is sometimes called the wise teacher or taskmaster of astrology, symbolising lessons learnt and limitations, showing us the value of determination, tenacity and resilience.

Rules the sign of Capricorn.

Jupiter

The planet Jupiter is the largest in our solar system and symbolises bounty and benevolence, all that is expansive and jovial. Like the sign it rules, it's also about moving away from the home on journeys and exploration.

Rules the sign of Sagittarius.

Uranus

This planet symbolises the unexpected, new ideas and innovation, and the urge to tear down the old and usher in the new. The downside can mark an inability to fit in and consequently the feeling of being an outsider.

Rules the sign of Aquarius.

Pluto

Aligned to Hades (*Pluto* in Latin), the god of the underworld or death, the planet exerts a powerful force that lies below the surface and which, in its most negative form, can represent obsessions and compulsive behaviour.

Rules the sign of Scorpio.

Neptune

Linked to the sea, this is about what lies beneath, underwater and too deep to be seen clearly. Sensitive, intuitive and artistic, it also symbolises the capacity to love unconditionally, to forgive and forget.

Rules the sign of Pisces.

The four elements

Further divisions of the 12 astrological signs into the four elements of earth, fire, air and water yield other characteristics. This comes from ancient Greek medicine, where the body was considered to be made up of four bodily fluids or 'humours'. These four humours – blood, yellow bile, black bile and phlegm – corresponded to the four temperaments of sanguine, choleric, melancholic and phlegmatic, to the four seasons of the year, spring, summer, autumn, winter, and the four elements of air, fire, earth and water.

Related to astrology, these symbolic qualities cast further light on characteristics of the different signs. Carl Jung also used them in his psychology, and we still refer to people as earthy, fiery, airy or wet in their approach to life, while sometimes describing people as 'being in their element'. In astrology, those Sun signs that share the same element are said to have an affinity, or an understanding, with each other.

Like all aspects of astrology, there is always a positive and a negative, and a knowledge of any 'shadow side' can be helpful in terms of self-knowledge and what we may need to enhance or balance out, particularly in our dealings with others.

Air

GEMINI ✷ LIBRA ✷ AQUARIUS

The realm of ideas is where these air signs excel. Perceptive and visionary and able to see the big picture, there is a very reflective quality to air signs that helps to vent situations. Too much air, however, can dissipate intentions, so Gemini might be indecisive, Libra has a tendency to sit on the fence, while Aquarius can be very disengaged.

Fire

ARIES ✷ LEO ✷ SAGITTARIUS

There is a warmth and energy to these signs, a positive approach, spontaneity and enthusiasm that can be inspiring and very motivational to others. The downside is that Aries has a tendency to rush in headfirst, Leo can have a need for attention and Sagittarius can tend to talk it up but not deliver.

Earth

TAURUS ✻ VIRGO ✻ CAPRICORN

Characteristically, these signs enjoy sensual pleasure, enjoying food and other physical pleasures, and they like to feel grounded, preferring to base their ideas in facts. The downside is that Taureans can be stubborn, Virgos can be pernickety and Capricorns can veer towards a dogged conservatism.

Water

CANCER ✻ SCORPIO ✻ PISCES

Water signs are very responsive, like the tide ebbing and flowing, and can be very perceptive and intuitive, sometimes uncannily so because of their ability to feel. The downside is – watery enough – a tendency to feel swamped, and then Cancer can be both tenacious and self-protective, Pisces chameleon-like in their attention and Scorpio unpredictable and intense.

Cardinal, fixed and mutable signs

In addition to the 12 signs being divided into four elements, they can also be grouped into three different ways in which their energies may act or react, giving further depth to each sign's particular characteristics.

Cardinal

ARIES * CANCER * LIBRA * CAPRICORN

These are action planets, with an energy that takes the initiative and gets things started. Aries has the vision, Cancer the feelings, Libra the contacts and Capricorn the strategy.

Fixed

TAURUS ✳ LEO ✳ SCORPIO ✳ AQUARIUS

Slower but more determined, these signs work to progress and maintain those initiatives that the cardinal signs have fired up. Taurus offers physical comfort, Leo loyalty, Scorpio emotional support and Aquarius sound advice. You can count on fixed signs, but they tend to resist change.

Mutable

GEMINI ✳ VIRGO ✳ SAGITTARIUS ✳ PISCES

Adaptable and responsive to new ideas, places and people, mutable signs have a unique ability to adjust to their surroundings. Gemini is mentally agile, Virgo is practical and versatile, Sagittarius visualises possibilities and Pisces is responsive to change.

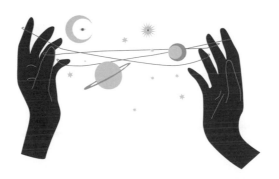

The 12 houses

The birth chart is divided into 12 houses, which represent separate areas and functions of your life. When you are told you have something in a specific house – for example, Libra (balance) in the fifth house (creativity and sex) – it creates a way of interpreting the influences that can arise and are particular to how you might approach an aspect of your life.

Each house relates to a Sun sign, and in this way each is represented by some of the characteristics of that sign, which is said to be its natural ruler.

Three of these houses are considered to be mystical, relating to our interior, psychic world: the fourth (home), eighth (death and regeneration) and twelfth (secrets).

1ˢᵗ **House**

THE SELF

RULED BY ARIES

This house symbolises the self: you, who you are and how you represent yourself, your likes, dislikes and approach to life. It also represents how you see yourself and what you want in life.

2ⁿᵈ **House**

POSSESSIONS

RULED BY TAURUS

The second house symbolises your possessions, what you own, including money; how you earn or acquire your income; and your material security and the physical things you take with you as you move through life.

3ʳᵈ **House**

COMMUNICATION

RULED BY GEMINI

This house is about communication and mental attitude, primarily how you express yourself. It's also about how you function within your family, and how you travel to school or work, and includes how you think, speak, write and learn.

4th House

HOME

RULED BY CANCER

This house is about your roots and your home or homes, present, past and future, so it includes both your childhood and current domestic set-up. It's also about what home and security represent to you.

5th House

CREATIVITY

RULED BY LEO

Billed as the house of creativity and play, this also includes sex, and relates to the creative urge, the libido, in all its manifestations. It's also about speculation in finance and love, games, fun and affection: affairs of the heart.

6th House

HEALTH

RULED BY VIRGO

This house is related to health: our own physical and emotional health, and how robust it is; but also those we care for, look after or provide support to – from family members to work colleagues.

7th House

PARTNERSHIPS

RULED BY LIBRA

The opposite of the first house, this reflects shared goals and intimate partnerships, our choice of life partner and how successful our relationships might be. It also reflects partnerships and adversaries in our professional world.

8th House

REGENERATION

RULED BY SCORPIO

For death, read regeneration or spiritual transformation: this house also reflects legacies and what you inherit after death, in personality traits or materially. And because regeneration requires sex, it's also about sex and sexual emotions.

9th House

TRAVEL

RULED BY SAGITTARIUS

The house of long-distance travel and exploration, this is also about the broadening of the mind that travel can bring, and how that might express itself. It also reflects the sending out of ideas, which can come about from literary effort or publication.

11th House

FRIENDSHIPS

RULED BY AQUARIUS

The eleventh house is about friendship groups and acquaintances, vision and ideas, and is less about immediate gratification but more concerning longer-term dreams and how these might be realised through our ability to work harmoniously with others.

12th House

SECRETS

RULED BY PISCES

Considered the most spiritual house, it is also the house of the unconscious, of secrets and of what might lie hidden, the metaphorical skeleton in the closet. It also reflects the secret ways we might self-sabotage or imprison our own efforts by not exploring them.

10th House

ASPIRATIONS

RULED BY CAPRICORN

This represents our aspiration and status, how we'd like to be elevated in public standing (or not), our ambitions, image and what we'd like to attain in life, through our own efforts.

The ascendant

Otherwise known as your rising sign, this is the sign of the zodiac that appears at the horizon as dawn breaks on the day of your birth, depending on your location in the world and time of birth. This is why knowing your time of birth is a useful factor in astrology, because your 'rising sign' yields a lot of information about those aspects of your character that are more on show, how you present yourself and how you are seen by others.
So, even if you are a Sun Gemini, but have Cancer rising, you may be seen as someone who is maternal, with a noticeable commitment to the domestic life in one way or another. Knowing your own ascendant – or that of another person – will often help explain why there doesn't seem to be such a direct correlation between their personality and their Sun sign.

As long as you know your time of birth and where you were born, working out your ascendant using an online tool or app is very easy (see page 108). Just ask your mum or other family members, or check your birth certificate (in those countries that include a birth time). If the astrological chart were a clock face, the ascendant would be at the 9 o'clock position.

The descendant

The descendant gives an indication of a possible life partner, based on the idea that opposites attract. Once you know your ascendant, the descendant is easy to work out as it is always six signs away: for example, if your ascendant is Virgo, your descendant is Pisces. If the astrological chart were a clock face, the descendant would be at the 3 o'clock position.

The midheaven (MC)

Also included in the birth chart is the position of the midheaven or MC (from the Latin, *medium coeli,* meaning middle of the heavens), which indicates your attitude towards your work, career and professional standing. If the astrological chart were a clock face, the MC would be at the 12 o'clock position.

The IC

Finally, your IC (from the Latin, *imum coeli*, meaning the lowest part of the heavens) indicates your attitude towards your home and family, and is also related to the end of your life. Your IC will be directly opposite your MC: for example, if your MC is Aquarius, your IC is Leo. If the astrological chart were a clock face, the IC would be at the 6 o'clock position.

Saturn return

Saturn is one of the slower-moving planets, taking around 28 years to complete its orbit around the Sun and return to the place it occupied at the time of your birth. This return can last between two to three years and be very noticeable in the period coming up to our thirtieth and sixtieth birthdays, often considered to be significant 'milestone' birthdays.

Because the energy of Saturn is sometimes experienced as demanding, this isn't always an easy period of life. A wise teacher or a hard taskmaster, some consider the Saturn effect as 'cruel to be kind' in the way that many good teachers can be, keeping us on track like a rigorous personal trainer.

Everyone experiences their Saturn return relevant to their circumstances, but it is a good time to take stock, let go of the stuff in your life that no longer serves you and revise your expectations, while being unapologetic about what you would like to include more of in your life. So if you are experiencing or anticipating this life event, embrace and work with it because what you learn now – about yourself, mainly – is worth knowing, however turbulent it might be, and can pay dividends in how you manage the next 28 years!

Mercury retrograde

Even those with little interest in astrology often take notice when the planet Mercury is retrograde. Astrologically, retrogrades are periods when planets are stationary but, as we continue to move forwards, Mercury 'appears' to move backwards. There is a shadow period either side of a retrograde period, when it could be said to be slowing down or speeding up, which can also be a little turbulent. Generally speaking, the advice is not to make any important moves related to communication on a retrograde and, even if a decision is made, know that it's likely to change.

Given that Mercury is the planet of communication, you can immediately see why there are concerns about its retrograde status and its link to communication failures – of the old-fashioned sort when the post office loses a letter, or the more modern technological variety when your computer crashes

– causing problems. Mercury retrograde can also affect travel, with delays in flights or train times, traffic jams or collisions. Mercury also influences personal communications: listening, speaking, being heard (or not), and can cause confusion or arguments. It can also affect more formal agreements, like contracts between buyer and seller.

These retrograde periods occur three to four times a year, lasting for roughly three weeks, with a shadow period either side. The dates in which it happens also mean it occurs within a specific astrological sign. If, for example, it occurs between 25 October and 15 November, its effect would be linked to the characteristics of Scorpio. In addition, those Sun sign Scorpios, or those with Scorpio in significant placements in their chart, may also experience a greater effect.

Mercury retrograde dates are easy to find from an astrological table, or ephemeris, and online. These can be used in order to avoid planning events that might be affected around these times. How Mercury retrograde may affect you more personally requires knowledge of your birth chart and an understanding of its more specific combination of influences with the signs and planets in your chart.

If you are going to weather a Mercury retrograde more easily, be aware that glitches can occur so, to some extent, expect delays and double-check details. Stay positive if postponements occur and consider this period an opportunity to slow down, review or reconsider ideas in your business or your personal life. Use the time to correct mistakes or reshape plans, preparing for when any stuck energy can shift and you can move forward again more smoothly.

Further reading

Astrology Decoded (2013) by Sue Merlyn Farebrother; published by Rider

Astrology for Dummies (2007) by Rae Orion; published by Wiley Publishing

Chart Interpretation Handbook: Guidelines for Understanding the Essentials of the Birth Chart (1990) by Stephen Arroyo; published by CRCS Publications

Jung's Studies in Astrology (2018) by Liz Greene; published by RKP

The Only Astrology Book You'll Ever Need (2012) by Joanne Woolfolk; published by Taylor Trade

Websites

astro.com

astrologyzone.com

jessicaadams.com

shelleyvonstrunkel.com

Apps

Astrostyle

Co-Star

Susan Miller's Astrology Zone

The Daily Horoscope

The Pattern

Time Passages

Acknowledgements

Particular thanks are due to my trusty team of Taureans. Firstly, to Kate Pollard, Publishing Director at Hardie Grant, for her passion for beautiful books and for commissioning this series. And to Bex Fitzsimons for all her good natured and conscientious editing. And finally to Evi O. Studio, whose illustration and design talents have produced small works of art. With such a star-studded team, these books can only shine and for that, my thanks.

About the author

Stella Andromeda has been studying astrology for over 30 years, believing that a knowledge of the constellations of the skies and their potential for psychological interpretation can be a useful tool. This extension of her study into book form makes modern insights about the ancient wisdom of the stars easily accessible, sharing her passion that reflection and self-knowledge only empowers us in life. With her sun in Taurus, Aquarius ascendant and Moon in Cancer, she utilises earth, air and water to inspire her own astrological journey.

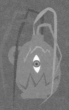

Published in 2019 by Hardie Grant Books,
an imprint of Hardie Grant Publishing

Hardie Grant Books (London)
5th & 6th Floors
52–54 Southwork Street
London SE1 1UN

Hardie Grant Books (Melbourne)
Building 1, 658 Church Street
Richmond, Victoria 3121

hardiegrantbooks.com

British Library Cataloguing-in-Publication Data. A catalogue record
for this book is available from the British Library.

Gemini
ISBN: 978178482655

10 9 8 7 6 5 4

Publishing Director: Kate Pollard
Junior Editor: Bex Fitzsimons
Art Direction and Illustrations: Evi O. Studio
Editor: Wendy Hobson
Production Controller: Sinead Hering

Colour reproduction by p2d
Printed and bound in China by Leo Paper Products Ltd.